A DAYDREAMER is PREPARED FOR MOST THINGS.

— Joyce Carol Oates

To bring anything into your life, imagine that it's already there.

-Richard Bach

FEET,
WHAT DO I
NEED YOU
FOR WHEN
I HAVE
WINGS
TO FLY?

—Frida Kahlo

Dare to live the life
you have dreamed for
   yourself.

   Go forward and
make your dreams
come true.
      - Ralph Waldo Emerson

KEEP SOME ROOM in YOUR HEART FOR THE UNIMAGINABLE.

-MARY OLIVER

PEOPLE ARE CAPABLE, AT ANY TIME IN THEIR LIVES, OF DOING WHAT THEY DREAM...

—Paulo Coelho

Dreams are ILLUSTRATIONS... FROM THE BOOK your Soul is writing about YOU.

—Marsha Norman